BOAS

DOUG WECHSLER

ACADEMY OF NATURAL SCIENCES

The Rosen Publishing Group's
PowerKids Press™
New York

For Seymour

About the Author
Wildlife biologist, ornithologist, and photographer Doug Wechsler has studied birds, snakes, frogs, and other wildlife around the world. Doug Wechsler works at The Academy of Natural Sciences of Philadelphia, a natural history museum. As part of his job, he travels to rain forests and remote parts of the world to take pictures of birds. He has taken part in expeditions to Ecuador, the Philippines, Borneo, Cuba, Cameroon, and many other countries.

Published in 2001 by The Rosen Publishing Group, Inc.
29 East 21st Street, New York, NY 10010

First Edition

Book Design: Michael de Guzman

Photo Credits: pp. 4, 7, 8, 11, 12, 16, 20, 22 © Doug Wechsler; p. 15 © Dan Nedrelo; p. 19 © Joe McDonald/CORBIS.

Wechsler, Doug.
    Boas / Doug Wechsler.
      p. cm.— (The really wild life of snakes)
    Includes index.
    Summary: Presents the habitat, physical characteristics, eating habits, and behavior of different varieties of boa constrictors.
    ISBN 0-8239-5603-2
    1. Boa constrictor—Juvenile literature. [1. Boa constrictor. 2. Snakes.] I. Title. II. Series.

QL666.O63 W427 2000
597.96—dc21   00-025720

Manufactured in the United States of America

CONTENTS

BOAS BIG AND SMALL

Boas are a group of snakes found in many parts of the world, especially in the **tropics**. The most famous boa is the boa constrictor, but there are many other **species**. Tiny sand boas are only a foot and a half long (0.5 m). The largest boa, the anaconda, can grow to more than 25 feet long (7.6 m). Some species of boas live in deserts, others in tropical forests. One kind, the rubber boa, lives as far north as British Columbia, Canada. It is about two feet (0.6 m) long.

The Bahama boa is a small boa from the Bahama Islands. Like most boas, it is usually active at night.

TREE BOAS, TOOTHY CLIMBERS

Most boas are good climbers. Tree boas spend most of their lives in bushes and trees. Several species of tree boas live in Central and South America. Tree boas are thinner than boa constrictors and are active at night. You can find tree boas at night by looking for the **eyeshine**. Like many creatures of the night, their eyes will reflect light from a flashlight and will seem to glow red. Tree boas have long front teeth that help them get a good grip on their **prey**. Their tails are **prehensile**. The tail grips the branch to keep the snake from falling. The front end of the snake catches and **constricts**, or tightens its grip around, the prey.

A young Amazon tree boa climbs a tree in Guyana, South America. Its tail grips the branch to keep the boa from falling.

SAND BOAS AND THEIR KIN

Sand boas and their kin are a group of chubby and short snakes. Their necks are almost as fat as their heads. Sand boas usually hunt in rodent tunnels. Sometimes they lie mostly buried in the sand and **ambush** mice that pass by.

Rubber boas and rosy boas live in western North America. The rubber boa looks and feels like rubber. Its tail is blunt, or rounded, like its head. Rosy boas live in rocky deserts. Like rubber boas, they are very gentle with people and almost never bite. People are not always as nice to boas. Rosy boas are rare in some places because so many have been collected as pets or run over by cars.

When in danger, a rubber boa, such as this one from the state of Washington, hides its head beneath its body. By doing this, the boa shows only its fat tail to the enemy instead of its hidden head.

ANACONDAS, MONSTERS OF THE SWAMPS

Female anacondas can be more than 20 feet (6.1 m) long. They are the heaviest snakes in the world. Females can weigh more than 300 pounds (136 kg). Males are much smaller. Anacondas live in South America and spend most of their time in or near water, especially swamps. They eat large rodents, small deer, turtles, and even **caimans**. There are scary stories about 50-foot (15-m) anacondas. Do not believe these stories. The longest ones found so far have not been longer than 25 feet (7.6 m).

Scientists studying in the marshes of Venezuela find anacondas by walking barefoot in the murky waters. They feel around for them with their feet.

Doug and his friend hold a 15-foot (4.5 m) anaconda in Ecuador, South America. Though they are powerful, anacondas do not usually attack people.

DOUG SAYS

BOAS, LIKE ALL SNAKES, HAVE NO EAR OPENINGS. WITH THEIR INNER EARS THEY CAN HEAR SOUNDS RUNNING THROUGH THE GROUND.

BOA CONSTRICTORS

The best-known boa is the boa constrictor. Few snakes live in as many different places as boa constrictors. They live in dry forests, rain forests, grasslands, and dry shrubby places. They are found in Mexico and in most of Central and South America. The boa constrictor eats many different things. Its diet includes rats, mice, **agoutis**, small monkeys, birds, and iguanas. Boa constrictors often grow to be 6 to 8 feet (1.8 to 2.4 m) long. A boa that is 12 feet (3.7 m) long is a giant. The record length for a boa constrictor is 18 1/2 feet (5.6 m).

This young boa constrictor from Belize, Central America, has found a nice resting spot in the gap of a boardwalk.

EGGS WITHOUT SHELLS

Instead of laying eggs as some other snakes do, female boas hold eggs inside their bodies. The eggs are well protected so they do not need shells. When the little snakes are fully **developed**, the mother gives birth to live young. Large boas usually give birth to more than 20 babies at once.

Each of the little snakes comes out of the mother in a clear **sac**. In minutes it breaks out of this sac. After it slides out of the sac, the little snake is on its own. The mother pays no attention to it. Though it is just a baby, it has everything it needs to **survive**.

Newborn boa constrictors, such as these, are born in clear sacs, not eggshells. Within minutes, they slide out of the sacs and are on their own.

DOUG SAYS

A TREE BOA CAN TELL WHERE ITS PREY IS EVEN WHEN IT IS TOTALLY DARK. IT SENSES THE HEAT WITH ITS PITS.

HOW DO BOAS FIND FOOD?

A boa uses all of its senses to find food. Smell is usually a boa's first clue to a good feeding spot. A boa flicks its tongue to gather tiny particles that smell. The tongue pulls back into the mouth. Inside the mouth a special **organ** works much the same as our noses do to sense smell. The boa follows the scent trail to a good place to wait, such as a rodent trail.

When the prey gets close, the boa can feel the prey's footsteps. It also sees the prey. The boa uses its tongue again to smell the prey. Tree boas can also feel the heat of warm-blooded animals with special organs called **pits**. Pits look like holes near the tree boa's mouth.

An emerald tree boa has heat-sensing pits near its mouth. The pits help the boa locate warm-blooded animals.

THE BIG SQUEEZE

The boa constrictor gets its name from the way it kills its prey. It constricts its meal. All species of boas kill their prey by constriction. When a mouse comes near a boa, the snake strikes. Almost in one motion, the boa constrictor grabs the mouse and wraps its body around it. The boa squeezes and tightens its hold each time the mouse breathes out. When the mouse stops breathing, the boa constrictor eases its grip. Supper is ready.

A boa constrictor kills a mouse by squeezing it. It wraps its body around the mouse and then tightens its grip.

EATING THE PREY WHOLE

To eat a mouse or other animal whole, it is best to start with the head. Otherwise the legs do not fold against the body and the animal will be too wide to swallow. A boa does not just look to see which end is the head. It flicks its tongue all over the prey to find the head. Next it starts to swallow, moving one side of its jaw forward and then the other. When only the mouse's tail is left sticking out of the boa's mouth, the boa raises its head and neck. Then the boa uses the muscles on the sides of its body to help push the mouse toward the stomach. The tail disappears down the hatch.

A Cuban black-tailed boa eats a Cuban tree frog. Boas start by eating the head first so the prey is easier to swallow.

ARE BOA CONSTRICTORS DANGEROUS?

There are many stories about boa constrictors attacking people. These stories are almost all made up. A boa will bite to protect itself if attacked or cornered. About the only people ever bitten are those who are trying to catch a boa. If a boa is ready to strike it will often hiss to warn the attacker to stay away. The bite of a boa is not poisonous. Do not get bitten, though. A boa's mouth is full of germs and germs can cause infection. A wild boa will try to constrict you only if you grab it.

GLOSSARY

agoutis (ah-GOO-tees) Rabbit-sized rodents of Central and South American forests.

ambush (AM-bush) To attack by surprise from a hiding place.

caimans (KAY-mens) Alligator relatives that live in Central and South America.

constricts (cun-STRIKTS) Squeezes. A boa constricts by coiling its body around the prey and squeezing.

developed (dih-VEH-lupt) To have grown.

eyeshine (EYE-shyn) The reflection of light from the eyes of an animal that is active at night.

organ (OR-gan) Any part of a plant or animal that does one certain thing.

pits (PITS) Sense organs on the face of a snake that detect heat.

prehensile (pree-HEN-sul) Adapted for grasping by wrapping around.

prey (PRAY) An animal that is eaten by another animal for food.

sac (SAK) A pouchlike part in a plant or animal.

species (SPEE-sheez) A single kind of plant or animal. For example, all people are one species.

survive (SUR-vyv) To stay alive.

tropics (TRAH-piks) The warm parts of Earth that are near the equator.

23

INDEX

WEB SITES

To learn more about boas, check out these Web sites:

http://www.mpm.edu/collect/boas2.html
http://www.belizezoo.org/zoo/herps/boa/boa1.html